POSTCARD HISTORY SERIES

Philadelphia
Historic Exteriors and Interiors

On the front cover: Taken in 1914, this photograph offers a panoramic view of the huge trimming department of the John B. Stetson Company in Philadelphia. The Stetson Company invented the ten-gallon hat that could actually be used by the cowboy to carry water. (Courtesy of author's collection.)

On the back cover: Please see page 81. (Courtesy of author's collection.)

POSTCARD HISTORY SERIES

Philadelphia
Historic Exteriors and Interiors

Gus Spector

ARCADIA PUBLISHING

ISBN 0-7385-4910-X

Published by Arcadia Publishing
Charleston SC, Chicago IL, Portsmouth NH, San Francisco CA

Printed in the United States of America

Library of Congress Catalog Card Number: 2006929703

For all general information contact Arcadia Publishing at:
Telephone 843-853-2070
Fax 843-853-0044
E-mail sales@arcadiapublishing.com
For customer service and orders:
Toll-Free 1-888-313-2665

Visit us on the Internet at www.arcadiapublishing.com

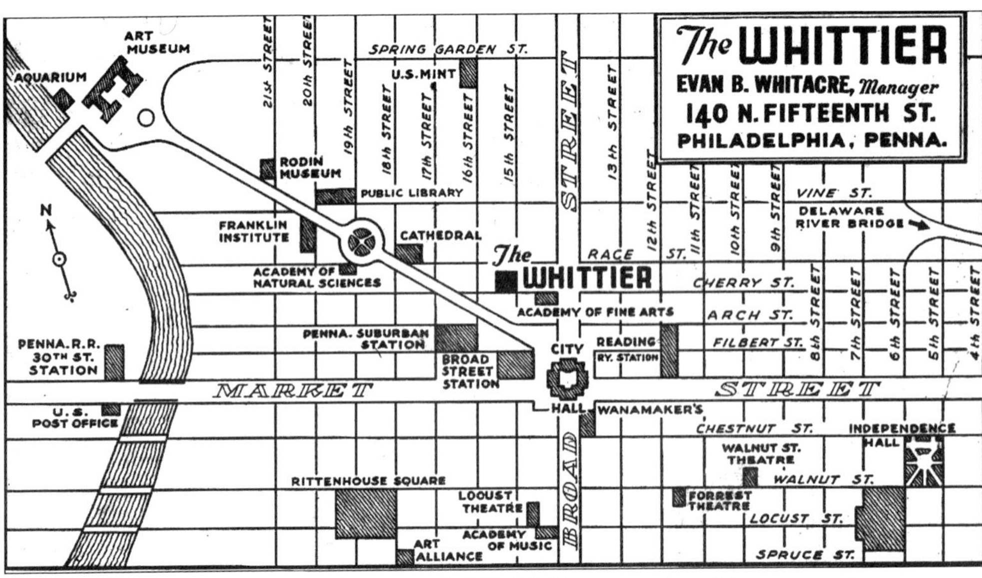

The Whittier Hotel circulated this map of Philadelphia as an advertising postcard.

Contents

Acknowledgments

Because of its wide range of local subjects, I have become a great fan of the Arcadia Images of America series. Through Arcadia, Vincent Martino Jr., author of three Arcadia books, and I have become friends (in spite of the many times that he outbid me on eBay!). On a cold, blustery weekend I had invited him to view my collection of Philadelphia postcards. "Gee, Gus," he exclaimed. "You've got a book here!" That was impetus enough to get me started. I offer my sincere appreciation to him for his time and patience in teaching me the technical skills necessary to make this book pressworthy.

My utmost and humble thanks go to Clarence Wolf, Philadelphia book antiquarian and historian. With his vast treasure of knowledge and good humor, he has graciously reviewed my text and assured me of not having made too many historical faux pas.

I also wish to thank my editor at Arcadia Publishing, Erin L. Vosgien. Answering my e-mails promptly and at all hours, she guided me through the production of this book.

Most importantly, this book is dedicated to my wife Karen, who, for many years, has tolerated my collecting interests.

INTRODUCTION

In producing a book composed almost exclusively of illustrated postcards it would be remiss not to include a short history of the postcard in the United States. The following is borrowed in part from John McClintock's classic *Postcard Primer.*

Private mailing cards began the postcard craze, and they spanned from 1898 to 1901. On May 19, 1898, an act of Congress permitted private publishers to print and sell cards that bore the inscription "private mailing card." The postage required for these cards was a whopping 1¢. Writing was not permitted on the address side, although some publishers left a small border on the view side of the card for a short message.

Hence the postcard era was born (1901–1907). This heralded the emergence of the real-photo postcard. Black-and-white photographs were printed on heavy paper stock with postcard backs. Itinerant photographers captured real-time street scenes and the flavor of life throughout Philadelphia. Writing was still not permitted on the address side.

The divided-back era spanned from 1907 to 1914. A printed vertical line down the middle of the reverse side of the postcard now allowed the address to be written on the right side and a message on the left. Many of the postcards in this book are from the period of time spanning 1898 through 1914.

The white-border era came next (1915–1930). The commonest and most plentiful postcards were printed during this time. A white border framing the view meant less ink expended by the printer.

The linen era spanned from 1930 to 1944. These cards were printed on paper with a high rag content. Although important historical events were recorded on linen postcards, many of the cards appeared cheap, flashy, and gaudy.

Finally came the photochrome era (1945 to present). Such postcards can be distinguished by their glossy "chrome" sheen.

In this volume I have attempted to avoid the duplication of the more common views seen in other books, and have focused on some of the unusual. Wherever possible, I have tried to link the exterior and interior views of the same subject to better illustrate the saga of old Philadelphia.

"Ah, yes!" quipped W. C. Fields. "Last week, I went to Philadelphia, but it was closed." Once the East Coast's leading industrial city, Philadelphia gained, after the dawn of the 20th century, the unenviable reputation of having morphed into a sleepy old town. In spite of its busy river ports, blossoming industries, and growth and development into a city of working-class homes, it was still regarded as a place where the sidewalks were rolled up at dusk. W. C. Fields also scoffed, "I once spent a year in Philadelphia, I think it was on a Sunday." This 1907 postcard typified the attitude of the times. However, as will be seen, Philadelphia *was* more than just a sleepy old town.

One

PHILADELPHIA'S FAMOUS STORES

Built in 1894 and seen here just after 1900, Gimbel's Department Store was a complex of buildings merged into one main Market Street store. Gimbel's introduced many department store firsts. In 1949, a metal charge-a-plate, a forerunner of the modern credit card, enabled shoppers to "shop without cash." The store had its own radio station, WIP. In 1945, the Slinky debuted in the Gimbel's toy department. All 400 Slinkys were sold out within 90 minutes.

Seen here is a glimpse of Gimbel's well-stocked grocery department as it was in 1904. The grocery specialized in delicious preserves and other gourmet items.

A panoramic view of the first-floor aisle revealed Gimbel's well-lit countertops overflowing with merchandise. An in-house crank-up telephone was used to converse with the store manager and other members of the sales force.

John Wanamaker, businessman, clergyman, philanthropist, and postmaster general of the United States, was author of the phrase "the customer is always right." His new department store opened in 1911, designed in the Italian Renaissance style by Daniel Burnham. Twelve stories high with three subbasement levels, Burnham's rendition of the building is shown in this early view.

Burnham's plan allowed for spacious aisles and display cases structured around a six-story-high great court. This 1915 view peered down upon its massive central area. The Grand Court Organ, the largest playable pipe organ in the world, was originally installed at the 1904 St. Louis World's Fair. Beginning in 1956, Wanamaker's entertained shoppers with its Christmas light show incorporating the organ into a festive musical and visual display.

Egyptian Hall, a mammoth auditorium that seated 1,800 people, was located on the second floor of the store. Public concerts were conducted by such notables as John Philip Sousa.

This 1911 view reveals a corner of Egyptian Hall set aside as a sales display for Wanamaker's magnificent collection of pianos.

The Lit Brothers store, built after 1898, was located at the northeast corner of Eighth and Market Streets. After the designs of Collins and Autenrieth, it was the first building in Philadelphia to sport a cast-iron facade. As was the fate of the other department stores on Market Street, Lit's could not compete with the national "big box stores" and was converted into the Mellon Bank Center in 1987.

Lit Brothers's Eighth Street subway window display was an eye-catcher even for the hurried shopper. An interview in the *Philadelphia Inquirer* stated that Lit's was "more working class. They had less frills, and the kind of sales depicted on the Lucy Show where ladies fought tooth and nail at the bargain tables and sales racks."

Quaker merchants Justus C. Strawbridge and Isaac H. Clothier opened their Market Street store in 1868, catering to "the better class of people." In the 1920s, men and women dressed in their finest flocked to live Saturday radio broadcasts in the store's WFI studio. When WFI later merged with Lit's WLIT, the call letters changed to WFIL. The store is seen as it celebrates its 50th year in business.

Strawbridge and Clothier featured wide aisles, mahogany counters, and plush ladies' restrooms. A 1903 birds-eye view of its dress-goods aisle is captured here. On May 23, 2006, Strawbridge's closed its doors. The *Philadelphia Inquirer* eulogized the store as being "as distinctively Philadelphian as Carpenters' Hall or the Betsy Ross House."

The Finley Acker Company was a family-run business. Opened in 1882 at Twelfth and Chestnut Streets, it specialized in confections, coffees, teas, olive oil, perfumes, cigars, and daily gourmet luncheons. The building's exterior around 1904 was a huge Italianate affair. The Finley Acker Company was last listed in the Philadelphia telephone directory in 1920.

Acker carried its elegant and ornately opulent motifs to the extreme. The display case in the foreground is filled with mouthwatering candies. The stylish overhang is beset with a long row of bare bulbs, as is its mirrored back wall. One would think that the great heat from the lighting would cause the chocolates to melt!

At the peak of its success, Leary's Book Store was reputed to have had over one million books in stock. Its seven stories housed six-and-a-half miles of shelf space. Leary's opened its 9 South Ninth Street location in 1876, directly behind Gimbel's Department Store.

Looking into the store's entrance, one might visualize only a minute portion of the vast array of books available for purchase. Although this photograph was taken in the 1950s, the look of its interior was basically identical to that of 1880. Leary's was forced to close in 1969, and the entire content of the store was liquidated at auction.

Two

Places to Eat and Sleep

The Bellevue Stratford, known as the Grand Dame of Broad Street and built at a cost of over $8 million, opened its revolving doors in 1904. It was designed in the French Renaissance tradition by George C. Boldt. The Bellevue immediately became the darling of the rich, royalty, and heads of state. The magnificent hotel dwarfs its immediate neighbors in this 1904 postcard.

The Bellevue's President's Suite, complete with period French provincial furniture and an upright piano, is seen in this 1916 view.

The breathtaking Bellevue Stratford ballroom was the scene of many important local and national social events. It is seen here in all of its glory in 1915.

The Great Depression wreaked havoc upon the Bellevue, and much of its glitzy trappings began to tarnish and fade. In the 1950s, the Bellevue ballroom was used for more mundane purposes, such as the Delaware Valley Square Dance Convention.

This 1950s postcard advertises "completely new, modern Barber Shop, designed for the Man of the Hour. Delightfully air-conditioned. Expert barbering—10 chairs, no waiting. Manicuring, bootblacking." There certainly appears to be "no waiting" when this photograph was taken!

The Lorraine Hotel looms menacingly today over lower north Broad Street, reminiscent of the Disney ride Tower of Terror. Designed in the French Renaissance Revival style, it was built between 1892 and 1894 as the Lorraine Apartments to accommodate the rich and famous. It was purchased by Father Divine and his followers in 1948 and was Philadelphia's first fully integrated four-star hotel.

The Lorraine's mammoth high-domed Chelsea Banquet Room had a seating capacity of 400. The banquet room was known for its excellent service and cuisine.

The Lorraine boasted 300 rooms, a restaurant, fireproof construction, and the modern amenity of two garages. In 1927, rates ranged from $2.50 to $3.50 per night. The main lobby was resplendent with handsome archways and marble columns. The hotel has been closed for many years and is currently for sale.

The Hotel Vendig was built in 1891, with alterations being made in 1928. It had the great advantage of standing at the intersection of Twelfth and Market Streets, directly across from the Reading Terminal. In fact, many early postcards of the terminal caught a glimpse of the corner of the hotel's facade. In a deteriorated state, it was demolished as part of the new Philadelphia Convention Center project.

Both for reasons of modesty and etiquette, the Vendig had, in its post-Victorian era, a separate ladies' dining room.

The reverse side of this 1930s linen postcard states "the finest Negro Hotel in the east owned and operated by a Negro, located at Broad and Oxford Streets. Miss Marie Patterson, Manager." The name on the hotel sign is unidentifiable.

The Soulas Hotel, located at 1337–1341 Arch Street near Philadelphia's Chinatown, was well equipped with many of the amenities of the time, including "all rooms with running hot and cold water, and many with private baths." Rates were $1 and up. In its better days, it serviced a clientele that worked in close proximity to Philadelphia's business district.

SOULAS HOTEL, 1337-41 ARCH ST., PHILADELPHIA, PA.

The Soulas Hotel's Altdeutsche Bierstube (Old German Beer Parlor) was adorned in heavy dark wood, typical of a German pub. Note the huge antlers masquerading as chandeliers.

In 1892, the Reading Railroad, memorialized forever in the Parker Brothers game Monopoly, was the country's largest rail system. The first train entered the Twelfth and Market Street terminal in 1893. Since that time the building has undergone numerous face-lifts. This 1909 postcard shows passengers in the terminal's lobby awaiting the arrival of their trains. The inset shows the building exterior as it was originally intended.

In 1948, a Sun Ray Drug Store and Horn and Hardart restaurant had been added to the facade. The Hotel Vendig still stood on the northwest corner of Twelfth and Market Streets. The corner site has more recently been radically altered by the addition of a huge neon guitar overhanging the Hard Rock Café. The Reading Railroad and its terminal closed officially on April 1, 1976.

The Reading Terminal Market opened on February 22, 1892. In 1938, unions attempted to organize the market's employees. By 1979 only 20 percent of the stalls were occupied. William L. Evans had, at one time, more than 50 stalls and an oyster bar. Evans sold his business to a vendor who closed in 1980. This 1950s-era card shows a section of Evans's well-stocked tables.

In this 1905 artist's conception, the Reading Terminal can be seen at far right. The Windsor Hotel was located at Twelfth and Filbert Streets.

Due to its proximity to the terminal, the Windsor was frequented by salesmen and visitors to the city. Here a banquet, held on March 7, 1906, had been arranged for merchants and travelers. Notice the Conestoga wagon centerpiece on the table.

Within the same block as the Windsor Hotel was located "The Venice" restaurant and bar, advertised on the postcard as being a "nationally famous 'old Philadelphia' landmark."

George Schott was the owner of Schott's Hotel, located near the Reading Terminal at Twelfth and Filbert Streets. Billy Penn could be seen perched atop city hall tower exclaiming "Meet me at Schott's Café."

Here, following Billy's instructions, one can "meet" in the interior of Schott's Café. This card was produced after the dawn of the 20th century by the Chilton Company.

Before the First World War, German cuisine and beer production exerted a profound influence upon Philadelphia's taste buds. This card, printed in 1898, shows the Green Room of the Charles W. Soulas Raths-Keller located in the Betz Building, close to city hall. The room was adorned with mounted deer heads and Teutonic weaponry.

The Soulas Raths-Keller's ladies' dining room was more formally equipped with crystal chandeliers and brass fixtures. But what happened to the ladies?

Harvey Ringler's Saloon at 632 Market Street had a highly polished bar. There were hanging towel racks on the customers' side of the bar, presumably for them to mop up their own spills.

Ostendorff's German Café and Restaurant, located at 1231 Market Street in the block later occupied by the Reading Terminal, was managed by L. Schmidt. Note the two gentlemen seated here appearing rather mellow. A huge rack of old German weapons and swords is displayed on the wall behind them, and a heavy brass spittoon rests at their feet.

The card states, "A jolly time at Peter's Rathskeller, northwest corner Germantown Avenue and Berks Street." Hopefully the card was correct.

Lew Tendler was "the greatest southpaw in ring history." The card shows a 25-year-old Tendler in 1923 posing in his fighter's stance. He died in 1970. Lew Tendler's, at Broad and Locust Streets across from the Academy of Music, was frequented by discerning gourmets and after-theater diners. Tendler's was known for its fine steaks and seafood. The landmark was demolished and has since been replaced by a parking garage.

Mention the name Horn and Hardart to anyone who had ever dined there and one will elicit an immediate smack of the lips. Known as the Automat, it was the creation of Joseph Horn and Frank Hardart. The Automat, opened in 1902, was the prototype vending machine. It was a cafeteria that displayed steaming hot food behind small pop-up glass windows that opened by dropping coins into its slots.

The Automat was especially popular during the Great Depression. The restaurant's "take out" logo was "Less work for mother." The chain remained in vogue through the 1950s, when its popularity diminished due to the advent of the fast-food restaurant. Horn and Hardart closed its last Automat in 1991.

Way back in 1912, in the days of inadequate refrigeration when one was only supposed to eat oysters in months containing an *r*, Frank and Rose Snock opened Snockey's Oyster and Crab House. They purchased their third place of business, an old ice-cream parlor at 523 South Eighth Street, shown in this postcard view, where they remained until 1975.

Snockey's long, narrow sparsely decorated Eighth Street location was constantly crowded with seekers of the finest seafood. Their current restaurant in the Society Hill neighborhood is much more spacious and sumptuous. Rose retired after 79 years and lived to be 95 years old.

Three

A City of Schools

In 1870, Thomas Richards, professor of architecture at the University of Pennsylvania, designed College Hall for the school's new West Philadelphia campus in Collegiate Gothic with a French mansard roof, utilizing serpentine stone. Cartoonist Charles Addams (class of 1934) had, on several occasions, posed the cartoon *Addams Family* in front of this Gothic dinosaur. College Hall is seen in this *c.* 1905 postcard.

In 1873, the university had a student enrollment of 759, and 486 of those were in the medical department. Thomas Richards designed Medical Hall in 1874 utilizing the same serpentine stone, not heeding warnings from the mineralogy department that the stone would not weather well. Both buildings have consequently needed frequent rehabilitation. Medical Hall was renamed Logan Hall in 1904.

This rare photograph was taken in 1904 outside of the Medical Hall's dispensary.

Thomas Richards's third Gothic study in serpentine stone was the Robert Hare Laboratory of Chemistry, completed in 1878 and named for the famous professor of chemistry.

Frank Furness, the most prolific architect of his day, designed the library. It was nicknamed the "glass palace" because of his concern over the amount of natural illumination within the structure. The library combined Romanesque arches and columns, Mozarabic massing, stone gargoyles, and art nouveau windows. Well ahead of his time, he designed moveable stacks so that, when necessary, shelf space could be increased tenfold.

Houston Hall, the first student union building in the United States, was constructed in 1895 based upon the designs of two students. Pictured here is the smoking room of the Houston Club. It was said that "Houston Hall is to the University of Pennsylvania what the Forum was to Rome."

One could only imagine what the appearance of this fancy *c.* 1900 dormitory room was like before it was cleaned up for this photograph!

The university swimming pool was 100 feet by 30 feet. Note the huge crowd of students hanging over the edges of the balcony.

The Mask and Wig Club has been in existence since 1894. It is the university's oldest dramatic organization and is off-campus on Quince Street in Center City Philadelphia. The murals in its auditorium were executed and decorated by a young Maxwell Parrish. The Grill Room remains basically unchanged to this day.

The student dormitories opened into five courtyards known as the Little Quad, the Triangle, the Big Quad, East Quad, and South Quad. Each dormitory entrance was given a historically based name, and a special door was designed for each. This was the dormitory entrance to the Robert Morris House by architects Cope and Stewardson.

Drexel University was the brainchild of financier Anthony J. Drexel. The school's curriculum included comprehensive studies in engineering and technical business training. The university's cooperative studies program allowed students to learn their didactic material and then, during the school year, put this into practice in a practical work setting.

Drexel spared no expense in creating his university building. Employing the architects Wilson Brothers and Company, the Chestnut Street side of the building was designed in the Renaissance style, the Thirty-second Street facade in a light buff brick with stained glass. Tall marble pillars, tiled floors, and reproductions of statues of the Italian Renaissance period graced the entranceway, giving the grand court a truly palatial aura. The main building was completed in 1891. Originally named the Drexel Institute of Art, Science and Industry, it was changed to the Drexel Institute of Technology in 1936 and to Drexel University in 1969. In 2002, Drexel University acquired the former Hahnemann University Medical School. A law school opened in the fall of 2006.

Temple University was founded in 1884 by Rev. Russell Conwell when seven motivated students wished to obtain a post-graduate education in the evenings while continuing their day jobs. By 1888, the enrollment was so great that the school applied for and received a state charter as Temple College. Temple remained a night school until 1891. College Hall, the first of its many buildings, is seen in this card, postmarked 1909.

Mitten Hall, built in 1931 as a student recreational facility, housed a large auditorium, cafeteria, and student lounge. Within an exterior niche sat a carved stone owl, the symbol of the school. This is a view of the building in 1937, as photographed by the prolific K. F. Lutz. A modern student facility is now on campus.

The interior of Mitten Hall appears rather cold and stark in this 1930s photograph. The furnishings have long since been upgraded, giving the main lounge a more comfortable appearance.

The Thomas D. Sullivan Memorial Library was built in the Gothic style with large ornamental windows being separated by buttresses. It opened in 1936.

The roof of the Sullivan Memorial Library reading room was supported by exposed hammer-beam trusses. Since the erection of Temple's modern Paley Library, the majority of the university's books and journals have been transferred there.

Completed in 1893, the Baptist Temple, designed in granite in the Romanesque style by architect Thomas Lonsdale, had a seating capacity of 3,000. Reverend Conwell was pastor of the temple for many years. College Hall is seen in this 1913 postcard to the far right of the Baptist Temple. The church was sold to the university in 1974.

This is the interior of the Baptist Temple as it appeared in 1911. The building includes impressive leaded stained-glass windows. Ninety foot trusses extended the length of the nave and supported the roof. Reverend Conwell's seminal night school classes were held in the basement. The Chapel of the Four Chaplains was later located in its basement as a memorial to the famous chaplains of the Second World War. For many years the Baptist Temple had served as a cultural and spiritual center for the people of North Philadelphia. In the mid-1980s, several of the temple's roof trusses failed and the building was closed. Rather than demolish it, Temple University plans to renovate the structure as a performance hall.

With the addition of the Departments of Theology, Law, Pharmacy, and Medicine, Temple graduated to a university status. This 1934 postcard shows the extent of the campus.

The Palmer School of Business was located in the Mercantile Library at Tenth Street above Chestnut Street. The typewriting class seen here is composed of young ladies. A female teacher presides over the class at the front of the room in this 1909 postcard. The typewriters were of the square upright design.

The Curtis Institute of Music was established in 1924 by Mary Louise Curtis Bok Zimbalist, mother of actor Ephrem Zimbalist Jr. The building was originally the mansion of banker George Childs Drexel. All students attend on full scholarship, and admission is extremely competitive. Former students include conductor Leonard Bernstein, composer Gian Carlo Menotti, and soprano Benita Valente.

The grilled door, radiator fixture, and vestibule in the Curtis Hall entranceway displayed the magnificent artistry of the iron crafters of the 19th century. This real-photo postcard, although unsigned, has all of the hallmarks of having been taken by the same photographer as the above exterior shot of the building.

The Philadelphia Normal School for Girls was located on the corner of Thirteenth and Spring Garden Streets. It was adjacent to the Lulu Temple, after the latter building was completed in 1904. Erected in 1893 and designed by Joseph W. Anschutz, it was patterned in the Italian Renaissance style with a facade of gray granite. It functioned as a teacher training school for young women.

A view of the normal school's botany class is captured here. Although appearing most primitive by today's standards, it was state of the art in 1918.

The Baptist Institute for Christian Workers is a handsome brick building still located in South Philadelphia at 1425–1429 Snyder Avenue, close to the Snyder Avenue entrance of the subway. It was built between 1911 and 1925 by architect B. R. Stevens and was placed on the National Register of Historic Places in 1983.

The Baptist Institute was a preparatory school whose mission was to send its graduates throughout the world to teach the gospel. This 1912 postcard depicts students in the costumes of the countries in which graduates were working.

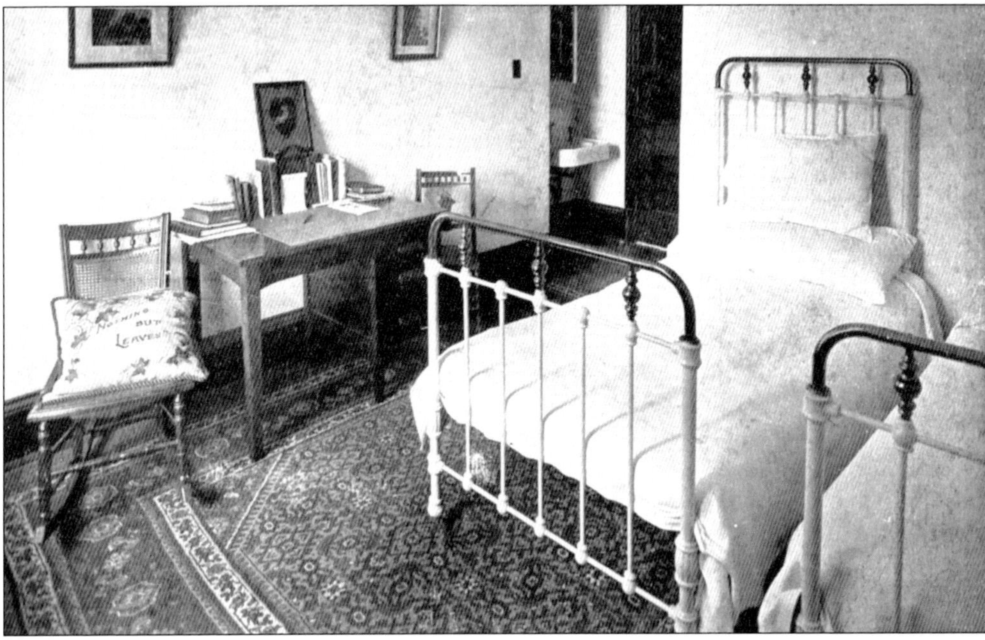

This card portrays a typical student's bedroom at the Baptist Institute for Christian Workers.

The entrance hall of the Baptist Institute appeared to be a warm, neatly appointed room.

The Baptist Institute's Margaret M. Tantum Library is shown in this card. The library shelves were not overly laden with books.

The main office of the institute is seen here. Has the gentleman seated at his desk been caught "asleep at the switch"?

Located at 1437 Snyder Avenue, just several doors to the west of the Baptist Institute, was the floral shop of C. B. Tustin. This real-photo postcard was published around 1914.

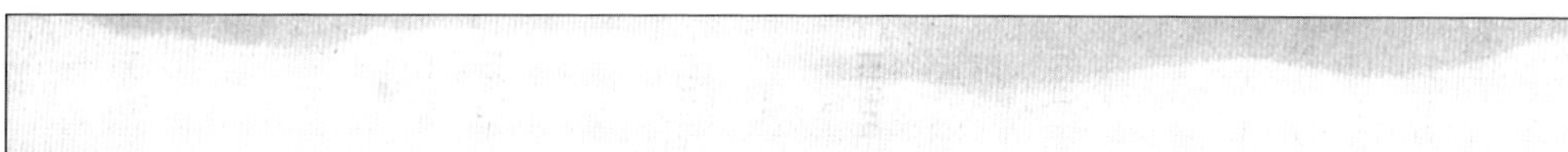

St. Joseph's House for Homeless Industrious Boys was located at Sixteenth Street and Allegheny Avenue, seen here around 1925. The conditions for admission to the school were that a boy had to be homeless or destitute, not "criminally inclined," had no relatives able to pay his support, had no guardian or relative to interfere with the boy's education, and that no relative could "remove an inmate unless certified by a clergyman."

Another requirement for admission to St. Joseph's House stated that the boy be between 11 and 14 years old. This view from the same set of postcards shows the students hard at work setting type in the printing department. The building was placed on the National Register of Historic Places in 1996. The property is now known as St. Joseph's Retirement Community.

Since Victorian times many institutions have promised to teach proper methods of public speaking and debating. This *c.* 1915 card shows the auditorium of the National School of Elocution and Oratory, located in the Parkway Building in central Philadelphia. (A mouth full of marbles, anyone?)

West Philadelphia High School is located on Walnut Street, between Forty-seventh and Forty-eighth Streets. It is the largest high school in West Philadelphia, encompassing an entire city block. It was completed in November 1912 at a cost of $1,126,700. One can only imagine today's comparable construction costs of a structure of such magnitude.

According to West Philadelphia High's current coeducational floor plan, there are "east" and "west" auditoriums. Before the school became coed, the boys' auditorium corresponded to the "west." In this 1914 card, one can see an ocean of apparently well-mannered young men, all sporting jackets and ties. The auditorium was massive, and the balcony overflowed with students as well.

This 1913 real-photo postcard provides an appalling view. The card is annotated, "This supplies West Philadelphia with gas. It is opposite the West Philadelphia High School." The huge gas reservoir was probably located in the open field seen in the right lower corner of the view of the school. Such a hazardous structure in close proximity to an urban school could well have been an invitation to catastrophe.

The E. K. Peall Conservatory of Music and Art was located at 3304 North Broad Street, near the Grand Opera House, when this postcard was sent in 1900. Besides teaching a full range of musical instruments, it also specialized in elocution and "impersonating languages."

The Philadelphia College of Pharmacy came into being in 1821 at a time when the sale and dispensing of drugs and medicines were in the hands of shopkeepers and charlatans. This card, dated 1900, shows the college building at 145 North Tenth Street. The college played a leading role in the standardization and updating of drugs and medicinals in the *U.S. Pharmacopoeia*, a reference book issued every 10 years.

The college was proud of its up-to-date equipment, which is seen in this early view of its pharmaceutical laboratory.

William Penn High School for Girls was located in North Philadelphia at Fifteenth and Mount Vernon Streets, near Broad and Spring Garden Streets. In 1929, its enrollment was 2,500. It had the same basic generic exterior found in any number of other Philadelphia schools constructed during the first decade of the 20th century. The card is postmarked 1914.

The structure of the auditorium was reminiscent of the real-photo postcard of the West Philadelphia High School auditorium seen on page 52. The card, entitled "Morning Assembly," relives the days when young ladies were encouraged to coif their hair in traditional styles and wear white blouses topped off with bows tied loosely about their necks.

Adhering to the old adage "a mother's place is in the home," these young ladies were being prepared for that fateful day when they would take their mothers' places in the kitchen. The card is titled "Cooking Laboratory."

This photograph by famous photographer William H. Rau was simply annotated "We Eat" and depicted the dimly lit overcrowded William Penn High School lunchroom. Lunchrooms of many of the schools of this era were located in the basements. The windows were of frosted glass covered by security wire, allowing very little light to enter.

Strayer's Business College was founded by Dr. S. Irving Strayer as a small Baltimore, Maryland, college in 1892. Its Philadelphia branch was located at 1109 Chestnut Street. The *c.* 1915 bookkeeping room looked like an ordinary classroom with uncomfortable wooden desks. Multiple fans were suspended from the ceiling of this well-lit classroom.

One third of the typewriting room is seen in this 1915 view. The typewriters were Remington models. Strayer University is still in existence, advertising 39 campuses and online degrees. In 1969, it received a license to grant the degree of bachelor of arts.

"Peirce means business" has been the motto of the Peirce Junior College since its inception by Thomas May Peirce in 1865. The Peirce School's third home at 917 to 919 Chestnut Street was in the Record Building. In 1915, the school moved to 1420 Pine Street, where it has remained to this day as an accredited four-year business school.

An enclosed rooftop exercise area in the Pine Street building enabled the Peirce School to offer classes in physical education. The city's skyline can be appreciated in the background.

Peirce Junior College decided to introduce typing courses in 1883. This 1920s view of one of the four classrooms in the new building was set with row upon row of desktop typewriters. In 1890, the school adopted the Benn Pitman system of "pen and pencil" shorthand. Extreme accuracy in both shorthand and typing were a prerequisite for graduation.

By 1891, the Pierce School also offered banking and business courses. Here the classroom of the banking department is seen.

EXECUTIVE-SECRETARY AND STENOGRAPHIC-SECRETARY COURSES

(University Grade)

The secretarial courses are designed to prepare young men and young women for secretaryships in institutions, financial and business houses, and with individuals, public officials, etc.

TEACHER-TRAINING COURSE

(University Grade)

Approved by the Dept. of Public Instruction of Pennsylvania. Graduates are qualified to teach commercial subjects in public and private schools. High-school education requisite for admission.

SALESMANSHIP COURSE

This course gives the student a general training for a business career, including the subjects of salesmanship and business psychology.

This is a portion of a 1920 postcard booklet detailing some of the preparatory courses offered by the school.

The Thomas May Peirce Public School at Twenty-third and Cambria Streets was named in honor of the founder of the business school, who died in 1896. The postcard is from around 1909.

Four

Before Medicare

In May 1751, the Pennsylvania legislature granted a charter to Dr. Thomas Bond and Benjamin Franklin to establish a hospital to care for the needy and the insane. The cornerstone was laid in 1755 at the intersection of Eighth and Pine Streets. This 1905 postcard shows the first building and its hospital grounds.

This 1905 real-photo postcard shows a view of Pennsylvania Hospital's clinical amphitheater, the oldest in the United States.

This early postcard reveals the fabulous double staircase in the hospital's entranceway.

In 1762, Dr. John Fothergill, a British friend of Franklin's, donated the first book to the hospital's medical library. The hospital now contains the first medical repository—and one of the largest—in the United States.

In 1871, Rev. Dr. E. D. Saunders conveyed his property in West Philadelphia, by reason of previous encumbrances placed upon it, to the Presbyterian Church. The church was to assume the debt and establish and maintain a Presbyterian hospital. This *c.* 1903 undivided-back postcard shows the Administration Building constructed in 1891.

The first 45-bed ward was erected in 1872 at Thirty-ninth Street and Powelton Avenue. The hospital is seen in this real-photo postcard around 1902.

The children's ward at Thirty-ninth and Filbert Streets was presented in 1888 by Mrs. John Wanamaker. It is shown here in 1905.

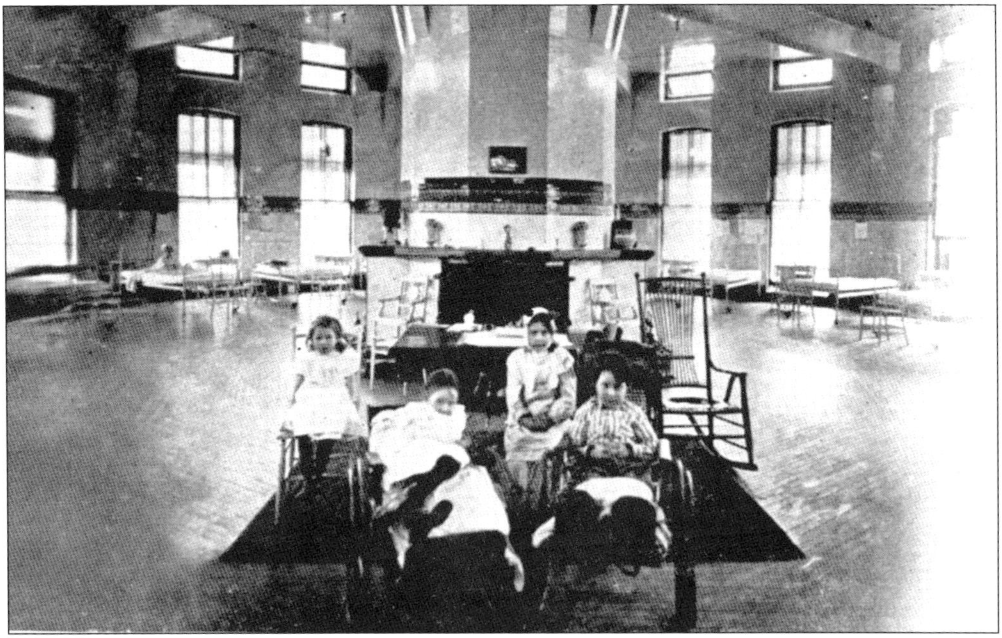

The interior of the Presbyterian Hospital's octagonal children's ward was photographed for this 1905 view. The room was large and spacious and had windows at each bedside.

The nurses' residence opened in 1899, having been presented by J. Renwick Hogg. The Training School for Nurses also opened in 1889, and within two months time "the first student nurses were put in charge of the women's surgical ward." Prior to the establishment of the maternity ward, student nurses received their obstetrical training at other hospitals. The first class, composed of eight nurses, was graduated in 1891.

In 1908, the medical staff of Presbyterian Hospital consisted of 64 practitioners, surgeons, and specialists. The hospital reported that it had been built, endowed, and supported solely through private funds, the only exception being an annual contribution made by the city toward its ambulance service. The majority of the bedding, bed linens, and clothing utilized within the hospital were provided by the hospital's ladies' aid society. The Maternity House alone, after opening in 1905, received 3,600 pieces of goods in that year from the ladies' aid society. In this early photograph, the maternity ward, which was endowed by an anonymous donor, is seen to the right of the large nurses' quarters.

By the beginning of the 20th century, the hospital had continued and increased its growth. This card is postmarked 1920, although the view of the Thirty-ninth Street entrance was probably earlier than that.

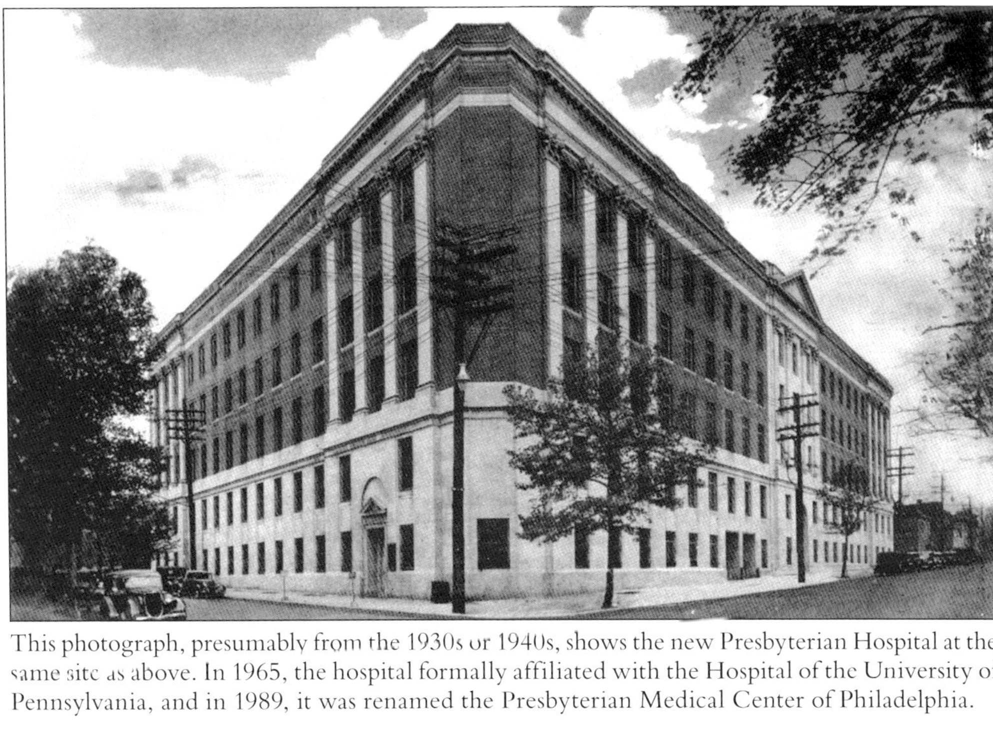

This photograph, presumably from the 1930s or 1940s, shows the new Presbyterian Hospital at the same site as above. In 1965, the hospital formally affiliated with the Hospital of the University of Pennsylvania, and in 1989, it was renamed the Presbyterian Medical Center of Philadelphia.

The Samaritan Hospital was founded in 1892 by Dr. Russell Conwell, first president of Temple University. A property was chosen at Broad and Ontario Streets and consisted of a sizable lot surrounding a large double house with 14 rooms, as seen in this 1903 view.

The dispensary was immediately flooded with patients, many of whom were indigent. There were men's and women's medical and surgical wards, as well as a gynecological service. The dispensary can be seen in this 1903 real-photo postcard. It is also visible at the rear of the hospital building as depicted in the previous picture.

When Temple College became a university in 1907, its medical department gained separate legitimate status. An affiliation between the medical departments of Temple and Samaritan Hospital and the Garretson Hospital greatly increased bed capacity to approximately 200. Physicians of the Temple medical faculty were the only doctors permitted on the staff of the Samaritan Hospital. Two nurses in full uniform are seen on the porch of the Home for Nurses. This new brick structure, erected in 1907 on the corner of Park Avenue, replaced an older building at Broad and Ontario Streets that had served as the original nursing residence.

Additional buildings were erected, finally culminating in the huge structure that became Temple Hospital. This real-photo postcard was produced around 1935.

This interior view is labeled "Main Lobby—The Samaritan Hospital of Temple University." Although the date remains unmarked, the photograph must have been taken prior to 1907, since the Samaritan Hospital was absorbed into Temple Hospital and the Samaritan name was dropped at that time.

On June 6, 1887, ground was broken for the Methodist Episcopal Hospital. The hospital, located at Broad and Wolf Streets in South Philadelphia, was founded and financed by a wealthy medical practitioner, Dr. Scott Stewart. This real-photo postcard shows the hospital when it was completed in 1892.

The architect Thomas P. Lonsdale, who also designed the Baptist Temple, drew up blueprints for the Methodist Episcopal Hospital utilizing a "pavilion plan," whereby there would be six separate ward buildings, each octagonal in shape. The plans had to be altered, and only one pavilion was actually ever erected. The pavilion can be seen on the left side of this 1912 card.

This is the interior of the octagonal-shaped women's ward in 1906. Note its similarity to the interior of the Presbyterian Hospital's children's ward, seen on page 65.

Hospital Day was celebrated on September 9, 1906. The attendant is seen standing alongside his horse-drawn ambulance.

In 1866, St. Mary's Hospital was located in "Fishtown," otherwise known as Kensington, in several buildings that had previously been a drugstore and a grocery store. The two adjoining original buildings can be seen in this 1903 undivided-back postcard.

In 1915, a fireproof hospital was built to replace the original. This 1916 postcard shows the "New" St. Mary's. The hospital has since been removed to more modern quarters, and the remaining building is now a nursing home and drug treatment facility.

St. Mary's nurses' training school opened in 1901, consisting of five sisters and six lay nurses. The nurses' residence was built in 1901 concurrent with the opening of the school. The comfortable lounge was furnished with deep soft chairs and adequate lighting as seen in this postcard from the 1920s.

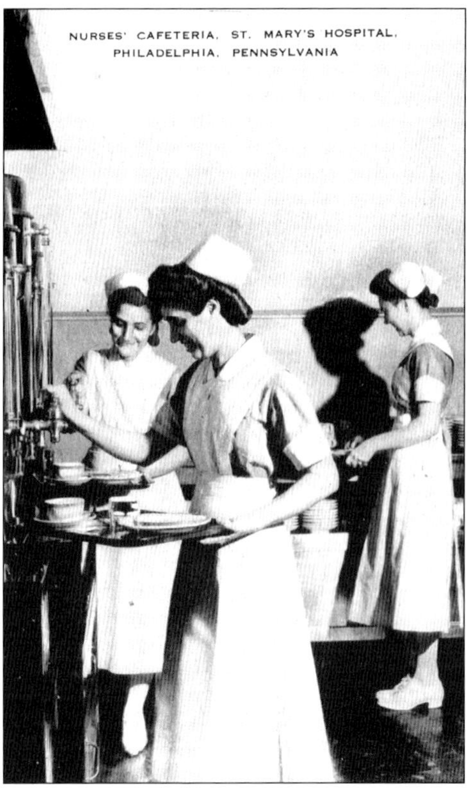

At the time that this photograph was taken around 1925, nurses were expected to wear the caps of their respective nursing schools at all times, even in the cafeteria.

When the Sisters of Mercy arrived from Ireland in 1861, they immediately initiated home visits to sick patients. The sisters founded Misericordia (Latin for "heart of mercy") Hospital in 1918 by mortgaging their motherhouse in West Philadelphia in order to afford the down payment. The site of the original property is captured in this view.

Nurses in full uniform are seen chatting on Misericordia's tennis court in this 1940s photograph.

This is a 1930s view of Misericordia Hospital, located at Fifty-fourth Street and Cedar Avenue in West Philadelphia.

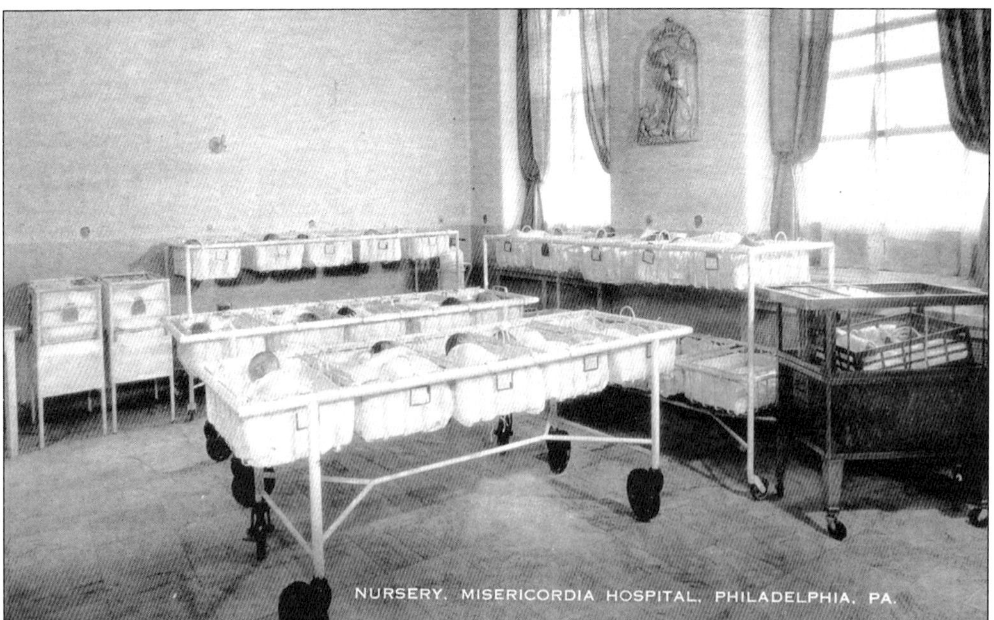

All of the bassinets are occupied in the Misericordia Hospital newborn nursery. There is no emergency medical equipment in evidence.

Five

PHILADELPHIA AND THE WARS

The war effort demanded volunteers. During World War I, an encampment was set up outside the north wing of city hall to recruit servicemen for "the Cause." The sign read "The Headquarters Train 200 Picked Men For Active Service." The Masonic temple is also seen (far right).

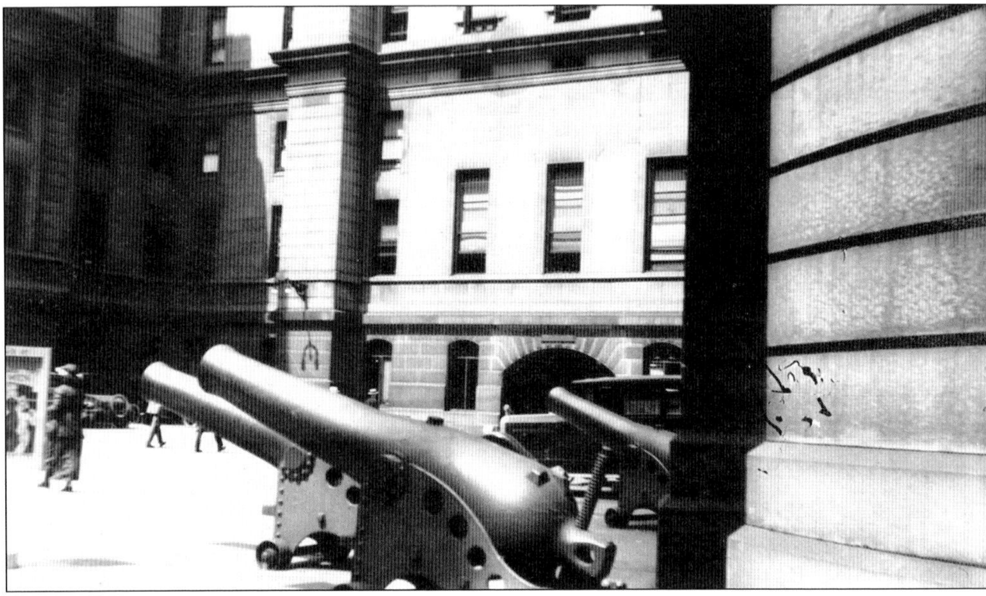

City hall courtyard served as a theater to display the might of America's fighting forces. Heavy cannon were in conspicuous view.

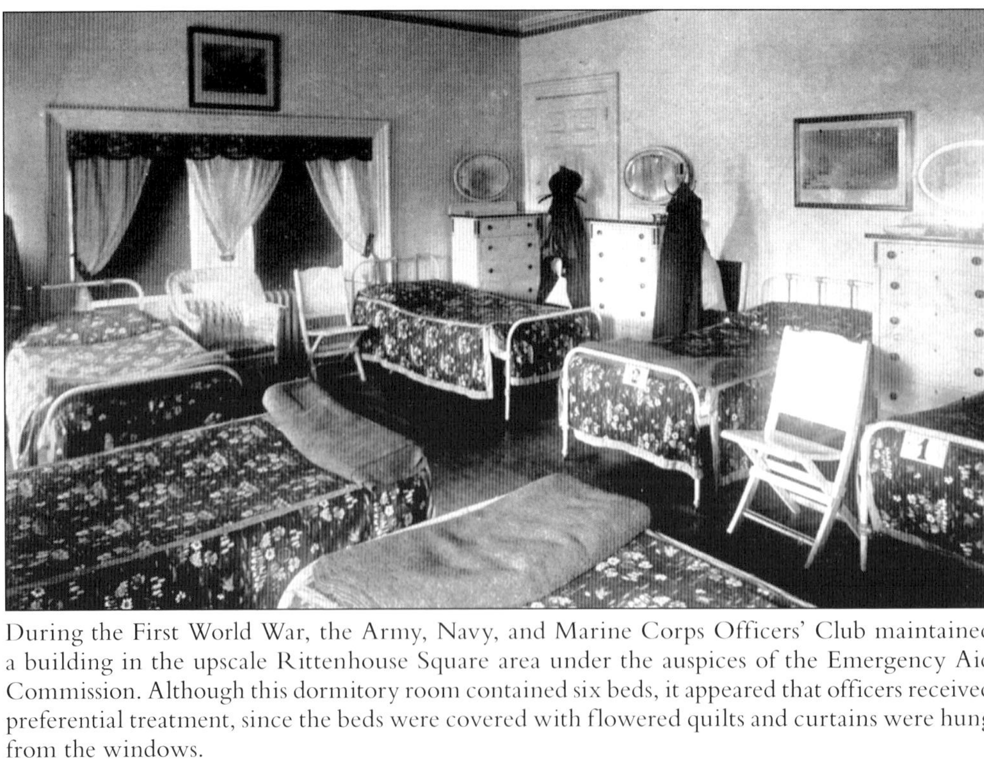

During the First World War, the Army, Navy, and Marine Corps Officers' Club maintained a building in the upscale Rittenhouse Square area under the auspices of the Emergency Aid Commission. Although this dormitory room contained six beds, it appeared that officers received preferential treatment, since the beds were covered with flowered quilts and curtains were hung from the windows.

A group of smiling officers enjoys a joke and a snack in the service officers' club cafeteria.

During World War I the Jewish Welfare Board maintained a building for its U.S. Army and Navy Philadelphia Headquarters in North Philadelphia at 1616 Master Street.

The Salvation Army's Servicemen's Hotel and Club was located at the Hotel Lorraine at North Broad Street and Fairmount Avenue during the First World War.

In 1941, Franklin Roosevelt approved the chartering of the United Service Organizations (USO), a conglomerate of the Salvation Army, YMCA, National Board of the YMCA, National Jewish Welfare Board, and the National Catholic Community Service. It was created for servicemen on leave away from home, providing facilities for dancing, movies, live entertainment, and religious counseling. The United Service Club was located at Seventeenth and Locust Streets, this card was postmarked in 1946.

Reyburn Plaza, a large city common, was the site of varied events such as free Philadelphia Orchestra concerts when World War II caused a serious decrease in concert attendance at the Academy of Music. Reyburn Plaza could be localized as the large open space along the lower edge of this postcard.

During World War II, Reyburn Plaza was officially known as the USO-Labor Plaza. It was maintained by the American Federation of Labor-Congress of Industrial Organization (AFL-CIO), in cooperation with the USO, United War Chest, and the City of Philadelphia. In this 1943 scene, soldiers and sailors gather to meet single young ladies at an outdoor evening dance.

The USO's Benedict Club was located at 157 North Fifteenth Street. Here servicemen are happily celebrating the New Year (1942) at a formal dance. This photograph is also currently posted on the USO's Web site.

The Hospitality Center for Service Men, 18 South Fifteenth Street, was under the directorship of the Recreation Committee of the Philadelphia Defense Council and the cooperation of the USO. This staged photograph shows an affable gathering of ladies and servicemen in a luxurious setting. The reverse of the postcard had no place for a postage stamp, having been pre-printed "Free" for use by service personnel.

The United States Navy first established a presence on League Island in 1876. During the Spanish-American War of 1898, the U.S. Navy appropriated better funding, and this primitive encampment grew into a small city. At the southernmost end of Broad Street, guards and gatehouses stood on either side of a flimsy gate. This undivided-back card is from around 1900.

As enlistees increased in number, more barracks were built, as well as facilities for social and religious activities. The Navy Red Triangle YMCA Hut was a prime example of this plan.

This postcard shows movie night in the Red Triangle Hut auditorium. Pity the poor sailor attempting to enjoy a movie while sitting far aft!

Sailors could release lots of pent-up aggression on the basketball court, also located in the hut.

Six

ORGANIZATIONS—OFFICIAL AND OTHERWISE

A card from the very early 20th century depicts this group of affable German gentlemen garbed in full regalia. Several men hold beer steins with the lids bearing the likeness of an owl's head. Their organization is unknown.

The Charlotte Cushman Club, located at Twelfth and Locust Streets, was named after the famous actress of the late 19th century. The club, founded in 1907, was a haven for "traveling women of the stage." Its dining room, pictured here, was known for its quality food. Women of the dramatic profession found it a compelling place to stay, since a light midnight meal was always available after their show.

Whenever a group of a particular nationality emigrates to another land, rather than initially assimilating into their new surroundings, they tend to live in close proximity to their fellow countrymen and establish societies reminiscent of those in which they participated in the old country. The German words *junger maennerchor* literally mean "young men's choir." Their building was located at the northwest corner of Sixth and Vine Streets.

This set of three postcards celebrated the 50th anniversary of their organization. The 1902 view shows both the ladies parlor and the banquet room.

The Maennerchor gave several major concerts each year as well as a number of smaller local performances. Their building therefore combined a rehearsal hall with other amenities, such as a billiard room.

The New Century Club at 124 South Twelfth Street was the oldest women's club in Philadelphia. It was organized in 1877 as an offshoot of the Women's Committee of the Centennial. Since married women were forbidden to own property in 1877, the charter application was signed by the group's single women. The drawing room, seen in this 1915 card, may not have been ample enough to accommodate the club's 600 members.

The women furnished the building with items taken from their own homes. This accounted for the truly feminine décor of the club's well-appointed parlor.

The club's name, New Century, was precisely chosen. During an era when women's rights were still debatable issues, the "new century" movement initiated the promotion of women's clubs on both local and national levels. The club offered classes in various aspects of modern domestic science. Sara Rorer taught Philadelphia's first cooking class at the club headquarters from 1880 until 1882. She realized that increased awareness of proper diet was an absolute necessity for good health. When she subsequently organized the Philadelphia Cooking School, it was a spin-off of the New Century Club. As can be seen in this early interior view, the club's lunchroom, where meals were prepared in-house, was well lit and commodious.

The Lulu Temple (or the Ancient Arabic Order of the Nobles of the Mystic Shrine) was profusely decorated in the Moorish style. The temple was dedicated in 1904 and was located at Broad and Spring Garden Streets. The huge green dome, surrounded by four smaller domes, was indeed an eye-catcher. This real-photo postcard was produced shortly after the temple had been erected.

The temple had a large auditorium, bowling alleys, a ladies' parlor, and a library. One of its meeting rooms, complete with all of its trappings, is viewed here.

The Philadelphia Young Friends Association was a Quaker organization founded in 1888. It erected a building at Fifteenth and Cherry Streets. The building, seen in this card postmarked 1907, was demolished in 1912. The Whittier Hotel was constructed in its place.

The Whittier Hotel provided rooms for long-term and visiting Quaker guests, as well as office space, committee rooms, and a restaurant. By the 1950s the building was no longer functional because of the Young Friends Association's new philosophies. It changed hands several times, and was sold to the Philadelphia Redevelopment Authority in 1971. This card is postmarked 1941.

The Whittier's lobby was simply appointed, in keeping with traditional Quaker ideals. It appears here in this 1920s view.

The auditorium, likewise, was most plain and unassuming.

Seven

AN INDUSTRIOUS CITY

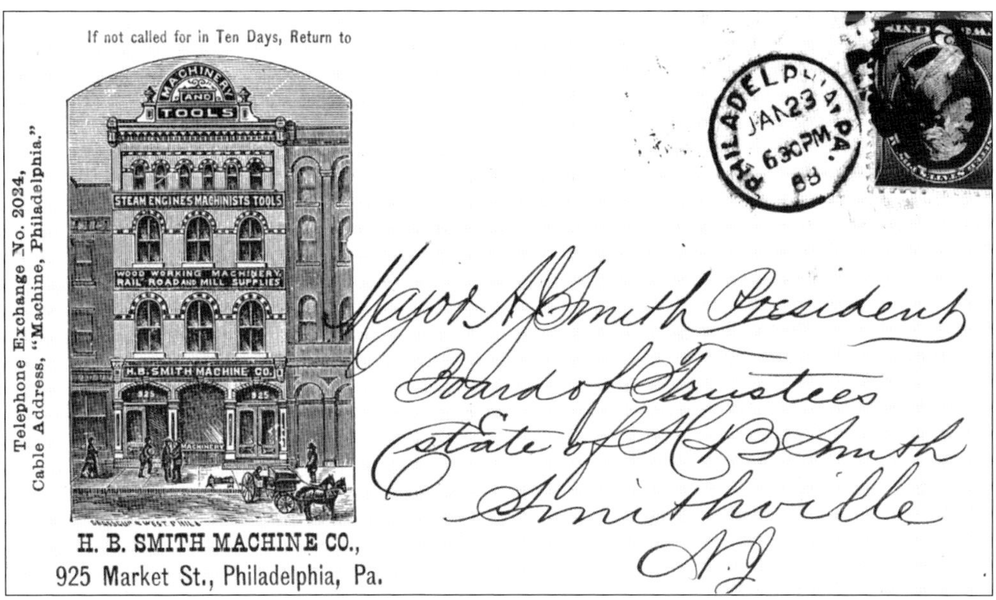

In the 1840s, Hezehiah Bradley Smith manufactured woodworking equipment as the H. B. Smith Machine Company. The company produced 150 different styles of machines and held more than 30 patents. At one time it manufactured one fourth of the nation's woodworking machinery. This illustrated envelope shows the company's 1888 manufactory at 925 Market Street.

The name and address stenciled on the side of this piece of equipment clearly identified it as having been manufactured by the H. B. Smith Machine Company. The real-photo postcard is undated, and the specific use for this machine remains nebulous and left to the reader's imagination.

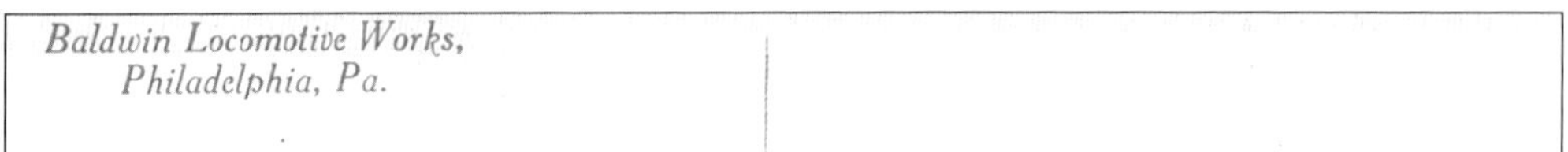

Matthias Baldwin produced his first locomotive engine, "Old Ironsides," in his shop at Fourth and Walnut Streets in 1832. As growing room was sorely needed, Baldwin moved in 1837 to a 20-acre site at Broad and Spring Garden Streets. By the 1880s, the company was producing 600 engines per year. By 1918, Baldwin had produced 50,000 locomotives. This is a 1915 view of the works, which was razed in 1937.

Servicemen sit on this open truck displaying a variety of different caliber artillery shells. The sign above them reads, "The Baldwin Locomotive Works. These will clear the way for the USA boys when they go over the top." The smaller sign reads, "The BLW Eddystone." Baldwin officially moved to Eddystone, Pennsylvania, in 1928.

In 1792, a structure at 35 North Seventh Street was emblazoned with the words "Ye Olde Mint." This became the first mint of the United States, and the first public building financed by the United States government. David Rittenhouse was the first director of the mint, having been appointed by Pres. George Washington. The building was demolished between 1907 and 1911, although this card was postmarked in 1908.

The second Philadelphia Mint, known as the "Grecian Temple," was erected at Chestnut and Juniper Streets in 1829. This postcard view was taken prior to 1888, since city hall in the background is seen before its tower was completed. The second mint could not keep up with the voluminous coinage necessary for a growing economy and was demolished in 1902.

The third mint was opened at Seventeenth and Spring Garden Streets in 1901. The architecture was that of a Roman temple facade, the glass in the vaulted ceiling designed by Tiffany. The view is that of the mint in 1931, with the Philadelphia skyline in the background. The mint closed in 1969 and now serves as part of the Philadelphia Community College.

The following set of postcards was produced around 1908. The complex steps necessary to produce a single coin were performed without the assistance of automated equipment. Seated at calibrated weighing scales is a crew of women determining the correct weight of various coins.

In 1900, the coin of the realm was the gold standard. The postcard portrays the refining of the gold.

This postcard states, "Weighing old coin. One million dollars in gold in sight."

In 1865, the John B. Stetson Company purchased a large plot of land in North Philadelphia at Fourth Street and Montgomery Avenue. Within a short period of time the company expanded rapidly and literally evolved into a small city, encompassing 30 acres of floor space and employing 2,500 men and 1,000 women.

In 1914, the Stetson Company produced a series of 12 advertising postcards graphically detailing their method of hat production. The reverse of each card provided commentary regarding the steps in each process. This card reads, "In the Fur Cutting Department 11.5 million skins are handled annually. The prepared skins are fed into the machines, which convert the pelt into fine shreds, the fur emerging apparently untouched."

"In the Forming Department the fur is blown on a revolving perforated copper cone. The cone and the felt are immersed in hot water, shaping the hat." This photograph is very graphic, and one could almost experience the noxious fumes wafting out of that unvented tank!

The Stetson Company provided its employees with many perquisites including a community of affordable housing and a hospital on the plant's premises. The employee Christmas party was celebrated each year in its enormous auditorium. When the wearing of men's hats was no longer stylish, Stetson was forced to close its Philadelphia plant. Today the Stetson Hat Company thrives in Garland, Texas, still producing the ten-gallon variety.

The name "Chilton" in the Chilton Printing Company was not a family name, but was chosen at random from the *Mayflower*'s passenger list. Although known as a publisher of auto trade journals, the West Philadelphia business, located at Forty-ninth and Market Streets, specialized in color printing. This 1918 birds-eye view of their plant was printed on their presses. The subway/elevated trains in the foreground commenced operation in 1907.

Chilton's Daylight Plant presses appeared idle at the time that this photograph was snapped. Printing prices quoted on the reverse of the postcard were $65 per 10,000, or $107.50 per 20,000 postcards. Chilton was responsible for printing many of the cards featured in this book.

The Weimer, Wright and Watkin Company manufactured and sold fine boots, shoes, and rubber footwear. Their building at 1210–1212 Arch Street was photoengraved on this 1907 envelope. The company produced "3W's Lenox Shoes" for young ladies and children; "Everybody's Shoes," leather shoes for women; and "3W's Dorcas Shoes," "hand turned shoes for comfort."

The 3W's Lenox Factory was a daylight facility with no recognizable overhead lights, fans, nor ventilation system. This card, dated 1911, was printed by the Chilton Company.

The Philadelphia Airport was dedicated by Charles Lindbergh in 1927 and was officially known as Municipal Airport in 1940. Until a proper terminal building was completed in Philadelphia, an airfield in Camden, New Jersey, was utilized. This postcard shows the single terminal and runway of the Philadelphia Municipal Airport. Note the sparse number of automobiles parked on its lot.

After the airport's completion, American, Eastern, Transworld, and United Airlines shared the single terminal. The airport was renamed the S. Davis Wilson Airport, then again the Municipal Airport, and then Southwest Airport before it received its permanent name. It appears in this photograph as the Southwest Airport of the late 1930s.

The airport's name was altered to Philadelphia International in 1945 when American Overseas Airways initiated flights to Europe.

The reverse side of this 1970s interior view of the airport states, "The Aero Gift Shop combines with the Horizon Grille to provide for the needs of the traveler."

The only logos recognizable above the ticket counters in this photograph are those of TWA and American Airlines. Notice the cigarette ashtrays situated in front of each of the service counters.

Eight

That's Entertainment

Columbia Park, located on a lot in North Philadelphia bordering Twenty-ninth Street and Columbia Avenue, was erected in 1901 at a cost of $35,000 with a seating capacity of 9,500. The ballpark was so small that the visiting team was forced to don their uniforms elsewhere and ride to the park via public transportation. The Philadelphia Athletics abandoned it for Shibe Park in 1908. The comment on the card is interesting.

Surely the names Shibe Park (1909–1953) and Connie Mack Stadium (1953–1976) bring back nostalgic moments to Philadelphia baseball fans fortunate enough to have attended games there. Shibe Park's original seating capacity was increased to 33,000 in 1925 when upper-deck and left stands were added. Residents of Twentieth Street sat atop their homes watching the games for free until Connie Mack added a high right field "spite" fence in 1935.

This card, dated 1919, shows the interior of Shibe Park, a capacity crowd in attendance.

Shibe Park's bleachers are packed to the brim in this 1912 postcard. Notice that every man is wearing a hat, which was quite the style of the time.

Franklin Field, located on the University of Pennsylvania campus, was built in 1895 at a cost of $100,000 for the running of the Penn Relays. The original low, horseshoe-shaped field, as seen in this 1904 postcard, was replaced by a two-tiered arena in 1922, making it the first double-tiered outdoor stadium in the country. The teams in the real-photo postcard are playing to a capacity crowd.

The arena originally known as Municipal Auditorium was erected in 1930. Constructed and decorated in the art deco style, it became well known for its classic friezes and other ornamentation. A portion of the now defunct Commercial Museum is also seen to the building's left.

Municipal Auditorium's name was changed to the Convention Center after having been host to the 1936 and 1948 Democratic National Conventions and the 1940 and 1948 Republican National Conventions. This view of one of the 1948 conventions well illustrates the massive ground floor teeming with delegates.

Sesquicentennial Stadium, constructed in South Philadelphia for the exposition of 1926, was built at a cost of $2 million and had a seating capacity of 100,000. The Jack Dempsey versus Gene Tunney heavyweight boxing match was held and broadcast from the stadium in that year. It is odd to see gondolas floating on an artificial lake in such close proximity to the stadium in this 1926 card.

A 1937 birds-eye view of the stadium reveals it to be surrounded by huge parcels of undeveloped land. Sesquicentennial Stadium's name was changed to Municipal Stadium between the 1930s and 1963, and then to John F. Kennedy Stadium in 1964. Philadelphia mayor Wilson Goode officially condemned the building in 1989, and it was demolished in 1992. The area is now the site of the Wachovia Center.

Keith's Theater at 1116 Chestnut Street, designed by architect Albert E. Westover, opened in 1902 as a vaudeville house. The theater had multiple majestic lobbies and reception rooms. In 1949, it was rehabilitated into a movie house and finally demolished in 1971. Ada Reeve, whose name is emblazoned on the marquee, was a musical comedy star and a vaudeville headliner.

Keith's entire magnificently adorned theater entrance, including the freestanding box office, was open to the street.

Kiralfy's Alhambra Palace at Broad and Spruce Streets opened in 1876 just in time for the centennial crowds. Architect Frank H. Loenholdt employed a Moorish design and utilized bright, gaudy colors. After the Kiralfys filed for bankruptcy, the palace was altered and reopened as the Broad Street Theater, presenting Shakespearean and other classic plays. Prices for Saturday matinee performances ranged from 50¢ to $2. The theater was demolished in 1937.

This postcard advertises Genevieve Hamper playing the lead of Juliet at the Broad Street Theater. A Shakespearean tragedian, she excelled in *Hamlet*, *Macbeth*, and *Romeo and Juliet*. She also performed on the silver screen between 1915 and 1923 in such films as *Tangled Lives* and *Unfaithful Wife*. Hamper was born in 1888 and died in 1971.

The Grand Opera House at Broad Street and Montgomery Avenue lay far afield from Philadelphia's theater district. Opened in 1888, it was created by architect George Plowman for the Betz Brewing Company. It catered to both legitimate theater and vaudeville. In a scene from the musical *The Old Homestead*, which was in its 26th annual tour, the "famous quartet of farm hands" was a highlight of the show.

Palumbo's dinner theater was popular not only for its food but for the quality of entertainers that it presented. Frank Sinatra, Tony Bennett, Dean Martin, and Bobby Rydell were regulars. In the 1940s and early 1950s, Palumbo's boasted four nightly floor shows. Frank Palumbo was an active and well-respected member of the Italian American community. In 1987, a petition was circulated to rename the West River Drive "Frank Palumbo Drive."

Philadelphia's Chinatown, located between Arch and Vine Streets and from Eighth to Eleventh Streets, was established long before the dawn of the 20th century. The restaurant Mei-Hsian Lou opened in 1870 at 913 Race Street. Lee Fong's Laundry, previously at this same site, was memorialized as being the first Chinese business in the area. Race Street, Chinatown's main thoroughfare, is seen in this early view.

Customers preferring a more Americanized version of Chinese food found the Golden Dragon at 1526 Market Street more to their liking. This was the scene of a massive restaurant overflowing with joyous well-dressed men and women donning their best flapper outfits. The reverse of the postcard advertised "Charlie Kerr's Orchestra is great."

The Sesqui-Centennial International Exposition opened on May 26, 1926, marking the 150th anniversary of American independence. In 1923, three hundred acres of marshland were graded, covered with topsoil, planted, and by 1926 miraculously converted into the Sesqui grounds. The exposition, however, was not the anticipated great success. Of the 50 million visitors expected, the gates tallied only 10 million. The weather spoiled the event, raining more than half of the time.

Viewed through a brick archway, High Street, now known as Market Street, re-created the colonial atmosphere of "olde" Philadelphia.

A world championship rodeo was held on the grounds of the Sesqui-Centennial Stadium.

The massive Palace of Liberal Arts and Manufactures featured the International Business Machines (IBM) corporation's display of business and accounting machines.

Seven states participated in Sesquicentennial exhibits, displaying their natural and agricultural products. Illinois' imaginative cultural extravaganza included a colorful theme created solely from corn on the cob. Now how corny could they get?

The government of Persia erected a replica of an ancient mosque, one of the most exquisite architectural features at the fair. The mosque's original doors were hundreds of years old.

Nine

All Vehicles were Once New

A magnificent Otto Fore Door Demi-Tonneau was parked proudly in front of General Grant's statue on the East River Drive in Fairmount Park. The princely prices of various 1912 Otto models were printed on the front of the card, and the reverse announced that the Otto Motor Car Sales Company located at Thirty-second and Walnut Streets was the sole distributor of these vehicles.

In 1910, the West River Drive had not yet been paved and was merely a dirt track. Automobile racing, a new spectator sport, brought wide-eyed throngs of fans to the Belmont Pumping Station to witness these high-powered vehicles.

A Chadwick automobile driven by Len Zengle was the winner of the above 1910 race. The vehicle, equipped with a Truffault-Hartford suspension system, easily outran all of the other 31 cars.

Each year the Fairmount Park Commission issued strict highway regulations enforced by the park police. Shown here is an early Fairmount Park Patrol vehicle. The reverse of the card reads, "Harry Fowler, Stableman. Sam Kulp, Patrol Driver. 1923."

The Wissahickon Drive, a most picturesque section of Fairmount Park, was also unpaved. In this posed 1901 view a driver has made a wrong turn into the Wissahickon Creek.

The Oakland was produced by the Oakland Motor Car Company of Pontiac, Michigan, between 1907 and 1909. This Oakland Model 35, parked in front of the Germantown Cricket Club in the Philadelphia suburbs, sold for $1,075. Oakland Motors was a division of General Motors Corporation from 1909 until 1931.

James Boyd and Brother, manufacturers of fire apparatus, were located at Twenty-fifth and Wharton Streets in the Grays Ferry section of Philadelphia. The reverse of this card reads, "We are strictly fire apparatus builders. We do not build pleasure cars or commercial trucks, but give our undivided attention to the fire apparatus business."

Ten

Miscellany—Some Real-Photo Postcards

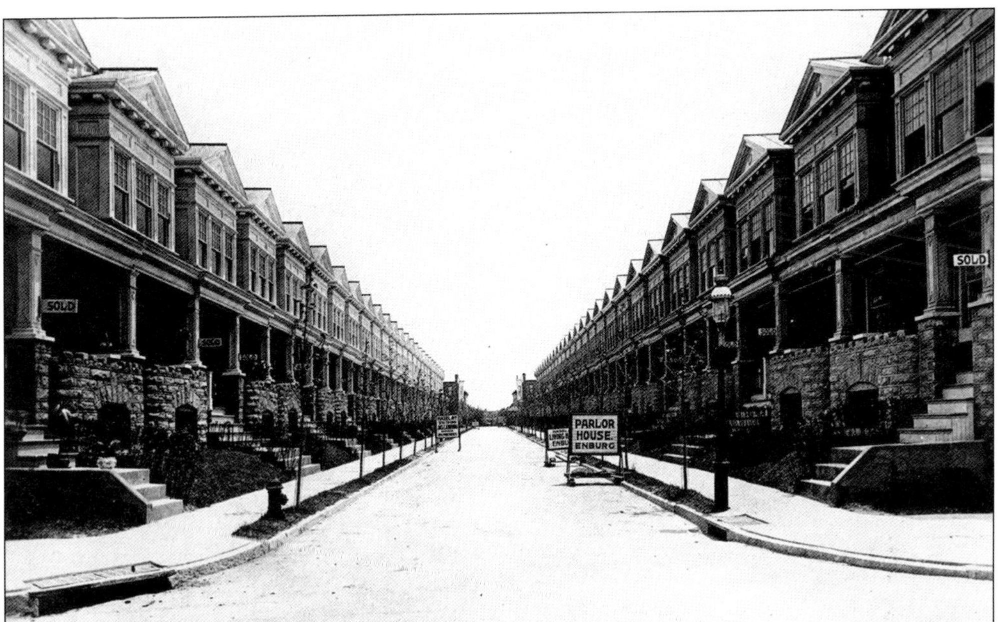

In the late 19th century, West Philadelphia's voluminous expansion was advanced primarily by the mass transportation industry. Huge tracts of farmland were converted into miles of homes within the price range of working-class citizens. Hazel Avenue, a newly completed street in West Philadelphia, was a typical example. Builder James Enburg labeled these "parlor houses." The 1911 postcard proclaimed "3 sold yesterday hurry if you want one."

In the early 1900s, itinerant photographers wandered the streets of Philadelphia, recording for posterity local events that they then sold as mailable postcards. All sorts of unusual real-photo postcards found their way into family albums. The date of this wintertime fire is unknown, but the image of spectacular formations of ice stalactites remains. The elevated train track seen on the right clearly places this somewhere on Market Street.

On January 13, 1912, a five-alarm fire struck the Lubin Film Exchange at 926–928 Market Street. The ice from water hoses coalesced on buildings and street as a result of the freezing temperatures and quickly became a grave hazard to the firemen. Eerily, this real-photo postcard was postmarked January 18, 1912, just five days after the fire was brought under control.

On May 14, 1914, a photographer recorded this accident at Sixtieth Street and Girard Avenue involving two Philadelphia Rapid Transit trolleys. The No. 15 car running westward on Girard Avenue was blindsided by a No. 44 car traveling south on Sixtieth Street.

A lad wearing a period Revolutionary War costume, surrounded by a bevy of young beauties neatly dressed in party clothes, is recorded in this photograph. A holiday celebration, perhaps the Fourth of July or George Washington's Birthday, was the occasion for this photo opportunity.

Between 1885 and 1915, the Liberty Bell was hoisted aboard a special rail platform and made a total of seven cross-country trips. Its last sojourn was to the 1915 Panama-Pacific Exposition in San Francisco. The bell, surrounded by appropriate ornamentation, is seen here photographed at one of its many stops along the way.

The famous house at 239 Arch Street rented by Betsy and John Ross between 1773 and 1786 was the site of their upholstery business and the place where Betsy sewed the first American flag. In 1898, concerned citizens donated their dimes to convert the timeworn building into a national shrine. This 1914 photograph shows the edifice's appearance after its rehabilitation.

With the advent of the automobile engine, jitney-like conveyances such as those used by "All Around Philadelphia" became popular tourist attractions. Passengers were packed tightly aboard open-air vehicles and transported all around Philadelphia. A photographer memorialized each trip by selling these personalized real-photo postcards.

In the 1850s, the William Penn Hotel located at Market Street above Thirty-eighth Street was an occasional meeting place for the Philadelphia City Troop. A mail stage traveled twice daily from the hotel to Newtown Square. The hotel burned in 1920 and was demolished in 1921. This 1907 view of the West Philadelphia hotel shows that it gave the neighborhood the appearance of an old frontier town.

The *Record* was one of Philadelphia's most prosperous daily newspapers. Its financial status deteriorated as a result of decreased advertising and labor union disputes. The paper was sold to the *Bulletin* in 1947. Huge throngs of sports enthusiasts would crowd in front of its scoreboard posted on the wall of the *Record*'s Ninth and Chestnut Street building. In 1905, it displayed up-to-the-minute football scores between the University of Pennsylvania and Lafayette University.

During the week of October 4–10, 1908, a grand citywide celebration marked the 225th anniversary of the founding of Philadelphia. An endless line of military regiments, police, firemen, and mystic organizations bedecked in their uniforms, as well as floats depicting historic events and the development of Philadelphia's industries, were memorialized in serial photographs by William Rau. The line of floats seen here certainly resembles rejects from a Rose Bowl parade!

Seen here is Philadelphia the city beautiful in 1907. Miss Philadelphia the beautiful was also photographed in 1907.

ACROSS AMERICA, PEOPLE ARE DISCOVERING SOMETHING WONDERFUL. *THEIR HERITAGE.*